New Hampshire Covered Bridges
A Guide for Photographers and Explorers

Published by Harold Stiver
Copyright 2012 Harold Stiver

License Notes

Version 1.0

Table of Contents

How to use this Book

For each of the over 50 Historical or Traditional Covered Bridges remaining in New Hampshire, we have included photographs as well as descriptive and statistical data. Traditional Covered Bridges are those that follow the building practices of the Nineteenth Century and the early part of the Twentieth Century or those built later that follow those methods. All of these bridges have had repairs done as portions wear out, and some may have been almost entirely replaced through the years. I have used "The National Society for the Preservation of Covered Bridges, Inc." list of what they consider as Traditional Bridges

Following is data included for each bridge

Name: This is listed in bold type, and where there are other names, it is the common name or the name listed on an accompanying plaque.

Other Names: Underneath the Common Name in brackets, you will find other names that the bridge has been known by.

Nearest **Township** and **County** are listed.

It is frustrating to go on an excursion to see something and not be able to find it. This book offers you multiple ways to ensure that doesn't happen.

GPS Position: This is our recommended method. Enter the coordinates in a good GPS unit and it should take you right there. You, of course, must use care that you are not led off road or on a dangerous route. In particular be careful you are not led onto a non-maintained road in the winter.

Detailed Driving Directions: Directions from a town near to the bridge.

Builder: If known, the name of the original builder(s) is listed.

Year Built: As well as the year built, if it has been moved it will shown with the year preceded by the letter M and, if a major repair has been done, the year will be shown preceded by the letter R.

Truss Type: The type for the particular bridge will be listed. If you are interested in more information on the various types of trusses, access "Truss Types" from the Table of Contents.

Dimensions: The length and number of spans.

Photo Tips: We try to give you some idea of what opportunities you have as well as restrictions, and special items you may want to incorporate into the picture. You may also find some useful ideas from reading "Photographing Covered Bridges" from the Table of Contents.

Notes: A place where you can find additional items of interest about the bridge.

World Index Number:
Covered bridges are assigned a number to keep track of them which consists of three numbers separated by hyphens.

The first number represents the number of the U.S. State in alphabetical order. Following number 50 for the 50th state are additional numbers for Canadian provinces. Thus the numbers 05 represents California.

The second set of numbers represents the county of that state, again based on alphabetical order. Humboldt is the 12th county alphabetically in California, and it is designated as 05-12.

Each bridge in that county is given a number as it was discovered or built. Zane's Ranch was the fifth bridge discovered or built in the County of Humboldt, California and it therefore has the designation of 05-12-05. Sometimes you will see the first set of numbers replaced by the abbreviation for the state, thus CA-12-05.

A bridge is sometimes substantially rebuilt or replaced and it then has the suffix #2 added to it.

National Register of Historic Places: If the bridge has been registered, the date is given.

Photographing Covered Bridges

Some standard positions

Portal: Taken to show the ends of bridge or bridge opening. This view, usually symmetrical, will include various signs posted. This is also a good way to get run over, so be careful!

3/4 view: Shows both the front and sides of the bridge, and is often the most attractive.

Side view: Taken from a bank or from the river, this gives not only a nice view of the bridge but usually allows for some interesting foreground elements.

Interior view: An image taken from the interior of the bridge will show some interesting structure but there is not a lot of available light. A tripod is important and HDR processing is helpful.

Landscape View: With the bridge smaller in the frame, you can introduce the habitat around it, particularly effective with colorful autumn foliage.

Using HDR(High Dynamic Range)

HDR is a process where multiple images of varying exposure are combined to make one image.

It has a bad name with some people because many HDR images are super-saturated, a kind of digital age version of an Elvis painted on velvet. However, the process is actually about getting a full range of exposure with no burnt out highlights or blocked shadows. This is an ideal processing solution for photographing Covered Bridges where you often have open light sky set against dark shadowed landscape and structure.

I use a series of three exposures at levels of -1 2/3, 0, +1 2/3, and this normally runs the full exposure range encountered. It is important to use a stable tripod.

One situation where you may need a larger series is shooting from within a bridge and using the window to frame an outside scene. The dynamic range is huge and you will need to have a series with a much larger range.

There are a number of software programs you can use to combine these images including newer editions of Photoshop. I use Photomatix which I have found very versatile and easy to use.

Best times for photographing bridges

Mornings and evenings are generally the best times for outdoor photography but the use of HDR processing makes it easier even in bright direct light. Although any season is good for bridge photography including the winter, fall foliage included in a scene can be spectacular.

A Short History of Covered Bridges

Let's deal with that often posed question; "Why were the bridges covered"

1. Crossing animals thought it was a barn and entered easily. I like this suggestion, it shows imagination. However, its not the answer although the original bridges normally had no windows and this is said to be because animals would not be spooked by the sight of the water.

2. To cover up the unsightly truss structure. I don't think those early pioneers were that sensitive, and personally, I like the look of the trusses.

3. To keep snow off the traveled portion. In fact the bridge owners often paid to have the insides "snowed" in order to facilitate sleighs.

4. It offered some privacy to courting couples, hence "kissing bridges". That is a nice romantic notion but no.

In fact, the bridge was covered for economic reasons. The truss system was where much of the bridge's cost was found, and if left open to the elements, it deteriorated and the bridge became unstable and unsafe. Covering it protected this valuable portion and the roof could be replaced as needed with inexpensive materials and unskilled labor.

Without coverings, a bridge might only have a life span of a decade while one that was covered often lasted 75 years or more before repairs became necessary. Besides extending the longevity of a bridge, wooden covered bridges had the virtue that they could be constructed of local materials and there were many available workers skilled in working with wood.

The first known Covered Bridge in North America was built in 1804 by Theodore Burr. It was called the Waterford bridge and it spanned the Hudson River in New York.

For the rest of the century and into the 20th Century, Covered bridge building boomed as the country became populated and people needed to travel between communities. The cost of constructing and maintaining a bridge was normally borne by the nearby community and many bridges charged a toll as a method of offsetting these costs. The period from 1825 to 1875 was the heyday of bridge building but near the end of that period iron bridges began to supplant them.

The number of Covered Bridges may have numbered 10,000 but have now dropped to about 950 spread throughout North America. Many have Historical Designations which provides them protection and many communities are interested in protecting their local historical bridges.

Carroll County
Jackson Covered Bridge
(Honeymoon Covered Bridge)

Township: Jackson
County: Carroll County
GPS Position: N 44° 08.499' W 71° 11.208'
Directions: In the town of Jackson take NH-16A/Mains St./Village Rd. east from the junction of NH-16 for 400 feet where you will see the bridge.

Crosses: Ellis River
Carries: NH-16A

Builder: Charles Austin Broughton and his son Frank Broughton
Year Built: 1876 (R1930) (R2004)
Truss Type: Paddleford and Arch
Dimensions: 1 Span, 121 feet

Photo Tip: is not a good side view but the 3/4 view is excellent.

Notes: There is a tradition of newlyweds having their photos taken in the bridge which gives it its alternate name. The pedestrian walkway was added in the 1930 renovation.

World Index Number: 29-02-01

National Register of Historic Places: Not listed

Bartlett Covered Bridge

Township: Bartlett
County: Carroll County
GPS Position: N 44° 05.675' W 71° 11.208'
Directions: from the village of Glen go west on US-302/Crawford notch/Main St for 1.4 miles and turn right onto Covered Bridge Lane where you will see the bridge.

Crosses: Saco River
Carries: Covered Bridge Lane

Builder: Unknown
Year Built: 1851 (R1966) (R1990)
Truss Type: Paddleford and Arch
Dimensions: 1 Span, 166 feet

Photo Tip: There is a good side view from the new bridge but be careful of traffic.

Notes: The building is presently a gift shop and there seems no problem in taking images of the bridge. In preparation for this, Milton Graton did the renovations in 1966. The gift shop owners also operate the B&B next door.

World Index Number: 29-02-02

National Register of Historic Places: Not listed

Saco River Covered Bridge

Township: Conway
County: Carroll County
GPS Position: N 43° 58.992' W 71° 06.983'
Directions: In the town of Conway go north on Washington St from the junction on Main St. and continue onto East Side Rd and you will reach the bridge after 0.4 miles.

Crosses: Saco River
Carries: East Side Rd

Builder: Charles Broughton and his son Frank Broughton
Year Built: 1890 (R1988)
Truss Type: Paddleford and Arch
Dimensions: 2 Span, 225 feet

Photo Tip: Good from all sides and a good river level side view from the south side.

Notes: This is the third covered bridge on this site. The first built in 1850 was destroyed when the Swift River bridge crashed into it in a 1969 flood. The second was destroyed in an 1809 fire.

World Index Number: 29-02-03#3

National Register of Historic Places: Not listed

Swift River Covered Bridge

Township: Conway
County: Carroll County
GPS Position: N 43° 59.066' W 71° 07.175'
Directions: In the town of Conway go north on Washington St from the junction on Main St. and continue onto West Side Rd and you will reach the bridge after 0.4 miles.

Crosses: Swift River
Carries: Bypassed section of West Side Road

Builder: Jacob Berry and his son Jacob Berry Jr.

Year Built: 1870 (R1890) (R1991)
Truss Type: Paddleford and Arch
Dimensions: 1 Span, 129 feet

Photo Tip: Easy from all sides. Look for a nice side view from the new bridge but watch for traffic.

Notes: The present bridge replaced one swept away in a 1869 flood. The Paddleford trusses have had a burr arch added at some point. The side are open from about 5 feet in height which gives it a light airy appearance.

World Index Number: 29-02-05#2

National Register of Historic Places: Not listed

Albany Covered Bridge

Township: Albany
County: Carroll County

GPS Position: N 44° 00.342' W 71° 14.473'
Directions: From the town of Conway go west on NH-112/Kancagus
Highway and after 6.0 miles turn right on Passaconaway Road
where you will see the bridge.

Crosses: Swift River
Carries: Campground entrance road.

Builder: Amzi Russell and Leandre Morton
Year Built: 1858 (R1982)
Truss Type: Paddleford and Arch
Dimensions: 1 Span, 120 feet

Photo Tip: Easy from all sides including excellent side views.

Notes: Located in the White Mountain national Forest, there is a $3
admission charge. The open sides, unpainted textured sides and red
roof make this a very picturesque bridge.

World Index Number: 29-02-06

National Register of Historic Places: Not listed

Durgin Covered Bridge

Township: Sandwich
County: Carroll County
GPS Position: N 43° 51.340' W 71° 21.866'
Directions: From the town of North Sandwich go north on NH-113A/Sandwich Rd for 0.8 miles and turn right on Fellows Hill Rd. and then after 1.4 miles turn left on Durgin Bridge Road where you will find the bridge.

Crosses: Cold River
Carries: Durgin Bridge Road

Builder: Jacob Berry
Year Built: 1869 (R1968) (R1983)
Truss Type: Paddleford and Arch
Dimensions: 1 Span, 96 feet

Photo Tip: Easy creek level side shots. The Paddleford and Arch system makes a nice image as well.

Notes: The 1968 renovation was done by Milton Graton and his son Arnold. The unpainted textured wood looks especially good in this natural setting.

World Index Number: 29-02-07

National Register of Historic Places: 09/22/1983

Whittier Covered Bridge
(Bearcamp Covered Bridge)

Township: Ossipee
County: Carroll County
GPS Position: N 43° 49.287' W 71° 12.738'
Directions: From the town of West Ossipee go northeast on NH25 from the intersection with NH-16 for 0.6 miles and turn right on Rudd Rd. and go to the end where you will see the bridge.

Crosses: Bearcamp River
Carries: Covered Bridge Road
Builder: Jacob Berry
Year Built: C1870
Truss Type: Paddleford and Arch
Dimensions: 1 Span, 133 feet

Photo Tip: Easy from all sides.

Notes: As of fall of 2012, this bridge was on blocks beside the river to be renovated.

World Index Number: 29-02-08

National Register of Historic Places: 03/15/1984

Cheshire County
Ashuelot Covered Bridge
(Upper Village Covered Bridge)

Township: Winchester
County: Cheshire County
GPS Position: N 42° 46.644' W 72° 25.408'
Directions: Found close to the town of Winchester, head west on NH-119/Hinsdale from the town and turn left on Gunn Mountain Road where you will see the bridge.

Crosses: Ashuelot River
Carries: Gunn Mountain Road

Builder: Nichols Montgomery Powers
Year Built: 1864 (R1999)
Truss Type: Town
Dimensions: 2 Span, 174 feet

Photo Tip: There are excellent setup points from all sides including some great 3/4 angle shots.
Notes: One of the finest covered bridges, it was built by one of the best builders, Nichols Montgomery Powers. It includes walkways on both sides.

World Index Number: 29-03-02

National Register of Historic Places: 2/20/1981

Coombs Covered Bridge

Township: Winchester
County: Cheshire County
GPS Position: N 42° 50.281' W 72° 21.649'
Directions: From the town of Winchester go north on NH-10/Keene Rd. for 4.0 miles and turn left on Coombs Bridge Rd. where you will see the bridge.

Crosses: Ashuelot River
Carries: Coombs Bridge Rd.

Builder: Anthony Coombs
Year Built: 1837 (R1964) (R1971)
Truss Type: Town
Dimensions: 1 Span, 118 feet

Photo Tip: There is a very good river level side view which will include some colorful foliage in the right season.

Notes: One of the state's older bridges, it is unpainted and the weathered front and sides look great.

World Index Number: 29-03-03

National Register of Historic Places: 11/21/1976

West Swanzey Covered Bridge
(Thompson Covered Bridge)

Township: Swanzey
County: Cheshire County
GPS Position: N 42° 52.303' W 72° 19.688'
Directions: In the town of West Swanzey find the bridge on Main St where it crosses the Ashuelot River.

Crosses: Ashuelot River
Carries: Main St

Builder: Zadoc Taft
Year Built: 1832 (R1998)
Truss Type: Town
Dimensions: 2 Span, 151 feet

Photo Tip: the detail on the portals make these shots interesting.

Notes: The bridge was closed in 1990 but reopen after 1998 repairs. It is characterized by a wide overhanging roof on the sides and includes a pedestrian walkway.

World Index Number: 29-03-04

National Register of Historic Places: 2/29/1980

Sawyer's Crossing Covered Bridge
(Cresson Covered Bridge)

Township: Swanzey
County: Cheshire County
GPS Position: N 42° 53.176' W 72° 17.173'

Directions: From the town of Swanzey go northwest on Sawyer's Crossing Road and continue for 1.0 mile where you will find the bridge.

Crosses: Ashuelot River
Carries: Sawyer's Crossing Road

Builder: Unknown
Year Built: 1859 (R1983) (R1996)
Truss Type: Town
Dimensions:2 Span, 158 feet

Photo Tip: Side views are not easy but can be found with care.

Notes: Nicely detailed, it is looking in great condition after the most recent repairs. There are side timbers acting as buttresses, probably to keep the bridge from twisting in wind conditions, something Town truss bridges are prone to.

World Index Number: 29-03-05

National Register of Historic Places: 11/14/1978

Slate Covered Bridge

Township: Swanzey
County: Cheshire County
GPS Position: N 42° 50.855' W 72° 20.411'
Directions: From the town of Winchester go northeast on NH-1-/Keene Rd and after 4.2 miles turn left on Westport Village Road. You will find the bridge in 0.9 miles.

Crosses: Ashuelot River
Carries: Westport Village Road

Builder: Unknown
Year Built: 2001 (Original 1862)
Truss Type: Town

Dimensions: 1 Span, 142 feet

Photo Tip: good views from all sides. The portal details are interesting.

Notes: The present bridge replaced an 1862 bridge which was destroyed in a fire in 1993. The bridge has red painted portals with white detailing and unpainted sides.

World Index Number: 29-03-06#2

National Register of Historic Places: 11/14/1978 (original bridge)

Carlton Covered Bridge
(Whitcomb Covered Bridge)

Township: Swanzey
County: Cheshire County
GPS Position: N 42° 51.277' W 72° 16.453'

Directions: From the town of Swanzey go south on NH-32/ Old Homestead Highway for 1.3 miles and turn left on Carlton Rd. where the bridge is about 0.5 miles.

Crosses: South Branch of the Ashuelot River
Carries: Carlton Rd

Builder: Unknown
Year Built: 1869 (R1996)
Truss Type: Queen
Dimensions: 1 Span, 67 feet

Photo Tip: Easy from all sides with especially good side views.

Notes: After recent repairs, the bridge looks excellent. It has a barn red exterior with some white detailing on the portals.

World Index Number: 29-03-07

National Register of Historic Places: 6/10/1975

Coős County
Happy Corner Covered Bridge

Township: Pittsburg
County: Coős County
GPS Position: N 45° 05.043' W 71° 18.814'
Directions: In the town of Happy Corner go south on Hill-Danforth Road off US-3 for 0.1 miles and you will see the bridge.

Crosses: Perry Stream
Carries: Hill-Danforth Road

Builder: Unknown
Year Built: 1869
Truss Type: Paddleford and Arch
Dimensions: 1 Span, 78 feet

Photo Tip: Side views are difficult due to foliage obstructions but you can get to water level with care. The bridge currently has strings of light on them which may look good in the dark but aren't helpful in the daytime.

Notes: The wood is unpainted and textured with wear and the sides are uncovered from about four feet.

World Index Number: 29-04-01

National Register of Historic Places: Not listed

River Road Covered Bridge

Township: Pittsburg
County: Coŏs County
GPS Position: N 45° 04.355' W 71° 18.340'
Directions: From the town of Pittsburg go east on US-3/Daniel Webster Highway for 5.9 miles and turn right on River Road where the bridge is found in 1.2 miles.

Crosses: Perry Stream
Carries: River Road (Bypassed)

Builder: Captain Charles Richardson or his son
Year Built: 1858 (R1954) (R1983)
Truss Type: Queen
Dimensions: 1 Span, 51 feet

Photo Tip: Found in a natural setting with good setups from all sides including a side view from water level.

Notes: An unpainted and well weathered structure open for half the height of the sides, it has extended portals, and seems to have had a number of recent minor repairs.

World Index **Number**: 29-04-02

National Register of Historic Places: Not listed

Clarksville Covered Bridge
(Pittsburg Covered Bridge)

Township: Clarksville-Pittsburg
County: Coős County
GPS Position: N 45° 03.280' W 71° 24.410'
Directions: From the town of Pittsburg go west on US-3/Daniel Webster Highway for 0.8 miles and turn left on Bacon Road where you will find the bridge.

Crosses: Connecticut River
Carries: Bacon Road

Builder: Unknown
Year Built: 1876
Truss Type: Paddleford and Arch
Dimensions: 1 Span, 89 feet

Photo Tip: There are excellent views all around and a particularly nice 3/4 view which takes advantage of the line of the guardrail and the background foliage.

Notes: This bridge lies on the line between Clarksville and Pittsburg townships and apparently this has cause some friction regarding paying the upkeep on this structure.

World Index Number: 29-04-03

National Register of Historic Places: Not listed

Groveton Covered Bridge

Township: Northumberland
County: Coős County

GPS Position: N 44° 35.749' W 71° 30.684'
Directions: In the town of Groveton take US-3/Lancaster Rd/Main St through the center of town and as it crosses the Upper Ammonoosuc River you will find the bridge on a bypassed section.

Crosses: Upper Ammonoosuc River

Carries: Bypassed section of US-3

Builder: Captain Charles Richardson and his son
Year Built: 1852 (R1965)
Truss Type: Paddleford and Arch
Dimensions: 1 Span, 126 feet

Photo Tip: This bridge is easy to photograph from all sides. Look for wildflowers to use as a foreground element.

Notes: It is painted white throughout and looks excellent. Milton Graton did the 1965 restoration, something he talks about in his book "*Last of the Covered Bridge Builders*"

World Index Number: 29-04-04

National Register of Historic Places: Not listed

Stark Covered Bridge

Township: Stark
County: Coős County
GPS Position: N 44° 36.043' W 71° 24.464'
Directions: from the town of Groveton head east on NH-110/Berlin-Groveton Highway and after 5.7 miles turn left on Northside Road where you will see the bridge.

Crosses: Upper Ammonoosuc River
Carries: Northside Road

Builder: Captain Charles Richardson or his son
Year Built: 1862 (R ca.1890) (R1954) (R1983)
Truss Type: Paddleford
Dimensions: 1+ Span, 138 feet (Pier added)

Photo Tip: Easy from all sides. Have a close look at the detail on the portals.

Notes: Surrounded by historic buildings, including an 1869 school and an 1853 church, it is an interesting spot to spend some time. It is a beautiful structure with two pedestrian walkways.

World Index Number: 29-04-05

National Register of Historic Places: 12/8/1983

Mechanic Street Covered Bridge

Township: Lancaster
County: Coös County
GPS Position: N 44° 29.194' W 71° 33.869'
Directions: In the town of Lancaster take Mechanic Street east from US-3 and the bridge is 500 feet.

Crosses: Israel River
Carries: Mechanic Street

Builder: Unknown
Year Built: 1862 (R1867) (R2007)
Truss Type: Paddleford
Dimensions: 1 Span, 94 feet

Photo Tip: Excellent views from all sides including an excellent side view.

Notes: An interesting aspect of this bridge are the graceful sweeping lines of the portals which extend over the sides. The sides are open for half the height.

World Index Number: 29-04-06

National Register of Historic Places: Not listed

Snyder Brook Covered Bridge

Township: Randolph
County: Coős County
GPS Position: N 44° 22.290' W 71° 17.332'
Directions: From the town of Gorham go west on US-2/Lancaster Road for 5.0 miles from the intersection with Main St. to a National Forest Parking Area. The bridge is found 0.2 miles on the old railroad right of way. from the information sign, a few steps will bring you to the rail right of way and you should go to the left.

Crosses: Snyder Brook
Carries: Abandoned Railway bed

Builder: Boston and Maine Railroad
Year Built: 1918
Truss Type: Boxed Pony Howe
Dimensions: 1 Span, 41 feet

Photo Tip: The best shots would seem to be from in front as well as a side view on the downstream side.

Notes: This bridge is known as a Boxed Pony. It has covered sides but not a top. This type is included in the "World Guide to Covered Bridges" and so we include them.

World Index Number: 29-04-P2

National Register **of Historic Places:** Not listed

Coös County and Essex County, Vermont
Columbia Covered Bridge

Nearest Town: Columbia, New Hampshire and Lemington, Vermont
County: Coös County, New Hampshire and Essex, Vermont
GPS Position: N 44° 51.159' W 71° 33.050'
Directions: Take Vermont-102 south from the Lemington are and turn left on Bridge St. The bridge is a short distance. From the New Hampshire side, take New Hampshire-26/ Us-3 south from Columbia and turn right on the Columbia Bridge Rd. and follow a short way to the end.

Crosses: Connecticut River
Carries: Columbia Bridge Rd.

Builder: Charles Babbitt
Year Built: 1912 (R1981)
Truss Type: Howe
Dimensions: 1 span, 146 feet

Photo Tip: There are good views from all sides, especially the north side in New Hampshire

Notes: This is one of three covered bridges which span the Connecticut River between New Hampshire and Vermont. It replaced a covered bridge which was destroyed by fire in 1911. There are full length sideboards on the downstream side and half length on the upstream. The theory is that during a flood, the force of the water will pass through the upstream openings and push off the boards on the downstream. The river is narrow at this most northern bridge between Vermont and New Hampshire.

World Index Number: 45-05-02 (Vermont) and 29-04-07 (New Hampshire)

National Register of Historic Places: December 12, 1976

Mount Orne Covered Bridge

Nearest Town: Lancaster, New Hampshire and Lunenburg, Vermont
County: Coős County, New Hampshire and Essex, Vermont
GPS Position: N 44° 27.634' W 71° 39.206'

Directions: From Lunenburg, Vermont take Us-2 east and turn right on River Road. After 0.3 miles, you will see the bridge entrance on the left. From Lancaster, New Hampshire go south on NH-135/ Elm St. and you will reach the bridge entrance in a bit more than 5 miles. You will not be able to walk or drive through the bridge as it is closed.

Crosses: Connecticut River
Carries: Mount Orne Road (Closed)

Builder: Berlin Iron Bridge Co.
Year Built: 1911 (R1969) (R1983)
Truss Type: Howe
Dimensions: 2 spans, 266 feet

Photo Tip: There are good views from the north side bank on both sides of the river

Note: This bridge replaced an open toll bridge built in the late 1800s. It was closed in 1983. It is said to produce a moaning sound in the right wind from the iron rods of its Howe truss.

World Index Number: 45-05-03#2 (Vermont) and 29-04-03#2 (New Hampshire)

National Register of Historic Places: December 12, 1976

Grafton County
Swiftwater Covered Bridge

Township: Bath
County: Grafton County
GPS Position: N 44° 08.074' W 71° 57.038'
Directions: from the town of Bath go southwest on NH-10/US-302/Rum Hill Road for 1.1 miles and turn left on NH-112/Wild Ammonoosuc Road and proceed for 2.1 miles. Turn left on Porter Road and you will see the bridge.

Crosses: Wild Ammonoosuc River
Carries: Porter Road

Builder: Unknown
Year Built: 1849 (R1947) (R1977) (R1989) (R1999)
Truss Type: Paddleford
Dimensions: 2 Span, 158 feet

Photo Tip: There are excellent side views from the rocks below but be careful. Good 3/4 view as well.

Notes: The bridge is unpainted except for a small amount of portal trim and looks nicely weather textured. The portals are shingled. Two previous bridges at this site were destroyed by floods but this one seems to have fairly high abutments.

World Index Number: 29-05-02

National Register of Historic Places: 11/21/1976

Bath Covered Bridge

Township: Bath
County: Grafton County
GPS Position: N 44° 10.007' W 71° 58.084'
Directions: In the town of Bath take Bath Road west off NH-10/US-302/Lisbon Road and the bridge is a short distance.

Crosses: Ammonoosuc River
Carries: Bath Road

Builder: Unknown
Year Built: 1832 (R1920) (R2007)
Truss Type: Burr Arch
Dimensions: 4 Span, 375 feet

Photo Tip: Go to the end opposite the town and you will gain easy access to the river edge. You will need a wide lens and might consider panoramic images. The church spire at the other side makes an interesting addition to the image.

Notes: This is one of the finest covered bridges in North America. Its setting is enhanced by waterfalls below as well as a typical white New England Church with spire at one end. Although this bridge has been here a long time, four previous bridges at this spot have been lost, three to floods and one to fire.

World Index Number: 29-05-03

National Register of Historic Places: 9/1/1976

Bath-Haverhill Covered Bridge
(Woodsville Covered Bridge)

Township: Bath-Haverhill
County: Grafton County
GPS Position: N 44° 09.252' W 72° 02.165'
Directions: In the town of Woodsville go north off US-302/ Central St. on NH-135/Monroe Road and the bridge is 0.3 miles.

Crosses: Ammonoosuc River
Carries: NH-135/Monroe Road (Bypassed)

Builder: Unknown

Year Built: 1829 (R1973) (R1980) (R2003)
Truss Type: Town and Arch
Dimensions: 2 Span, 256 feet

Photo Tip: Easy views especially an excellent interior. You can get good side views from the sidewalk of the new bridge beside it, you will need a wide lens.

Notes: This is a beautiful structure and while a sign on the bridge indicates it was built in 1827, it was not completed until 1829. This still qualifies it as the oldest surviving bridge in New Hampshire and New England. The Hyde Hall Covered Bridge in New York is the oldest surviving bridge in North America having been built in 1823. The most recent rehabilitation has the bridge looking excellent.

World Index Number: 29-05-04

National Register of Historic Places: 4/18/1977

Flume Covered Bridge

Township: Lincoln
County: Grafton County
GPS Position: N 44° 05.956' W 71° 40.599'
Directions: From the town of North Lincoln go north on US-3 for 4.4 miles to the entrance to the Flume Gorge, Franconia Notch State Park. The bridge is on an interior trail. There is an admission charge.

Crosses: Pemigewasset River
Carries: Pedestrian trail

Builder: Unknown
Year Built: 1871 (R1951)
Truss Type: Paddleford
Dimensions: 1 Span, 52 feet

Photo Tip: Don't take the shuttle as you will not stop at the bridge. There are good views from all sides although a bit obstructed.

Notes: This is a good family destination. There is a another pedestrian covered bridge called the Sentinel Pine as well as the attraction of the Flume River gorge.

World Index Number: 29-05-05

National Register of Historic Places: Not listed

Turkey Jim Covered Bridge (Destroyed by Hurricane Irene in Aug/2011)

Township: Campton
County: Grafton County
GPS Position: N 43° 51.142' W 71° 31.562'

Crosses: West Branch Brook
Carries: private Road

Builder: Milton Graton
Year Built: 1958

Truss Type: Queen
Dimensions: 1 Span, 61 feet

Notes: Destroyed by flooding caused by Hurricane Irene in 2011

World Index Number: 29-05-07#2

National Register of Historic Places: Not listed

Bump Covered Bridge

Township: Campton
County: Grafton County
GPS Position: N 43° 48.859' W 71° 37.315'
Directions: From the town of Compton go south on NH-175,
continuing on Perch Pond Road for 3.1 miles and turn right, staying
on Perch Pond Road and the bridge is 0.8 miles.

Crosses: Beebe River
Carries: Perch Pond Road

Builder: Arnold Graton
Year Built: 1972
Truss Type: Queen

Dimensions: 1 Span, 68 feet

Photo Tip: The side views are obstructed although you may find something passable when the leaves are off.

Notes: The Bump Bridge was built by Milton Graton in 1972 after he examined the previous bridge on this spot and found it could not be rehabilitated due to the deteriorated nature of its timbers. He gave the Town of Campton an excellent price of $2,500 to build it based on his being allowed to provide a bid to repair the nearby Blair Covered Bridge and this is what happened.

World Index Number: 29-05-08#2

National **Register of Historic Places**: Not listed

Blair Covered Bridge

Township: Campton
County: Grafton County
GPS Position: N 43° 48.616' W 71° 39.991'
Directions: From the town of Plymouth go north on US-3/Daniel Webster Highway/Main St for 3.2 miles and turn right on Blair Road where the bridge is a short distance.

Crosses: Pemigewasset River
Carries: Blair Road

Builder: Unknown
Year Built: 1869 (R1977)
Truss Type: Long and Burr Arch
Dimensions: 2 Span, 293 feet

Photo Tip: You can reach river level from the SE corner for a good side view.

Notes: This bridge was rehabilitated by Milton Graton and his son Arnold in 1977. The Long truss system had Burr Arches added. It is a beautiful structure with windows in each span giving it a nice balance.

World Index Number: 29-05-09

National Register of Historic Places: Not listed

Smith Millennium Covered Bridge

Township: Plymouth
County: Grafton County
GPS Position: N 43° 46.517' W 71° 44.359'
Directions: Take Exit 26 off I-93 and go west NH-3A/Tenney Mountain Road for 2.5 miles and turn right on Smith Bridge Road. You will see the bridge in 0.6 miles.

Crosses: Baker River
Carries: Smith Bridge Road

Builder: Stan Graton and Hayden Hillsgrove
Year Built: 2001 (Original 1850)

Truss Type: Long and Burr Arch
Dimensions: 1 Span, 167 feet

Photo Tip: There is an excellent 3/4 view from the viewing stand on the NE corner, and it is easy get to the river from the north side for a nice side view.

Notes: The original bridge was destroyed by fire in 1993. The replacement is an impressive structure which has a pedestrian walkway as well as two lanes for vehicles. It is built to carry interstate highway loads.

World Index Number: 29-05-10#2

National Register of Historic Places: Not listed

Edgell Covered Bridge

Township: Lyme
County: Grafton County
GPS Position: N 43° 52.055' W 72° 09.903'

Directions: From the town of Oxford go south on NH-10/Oxford Road for 1.6 miles and turn right onto River Road where the bridge is found in 0.9 miles.

Crosses: Clay Brook
Carries: River Road

Builder: Walter Piper
Year Built: 1885 (R1936) (R1971) (R1982)
Truss Type: Town
Dimensions: 1 Span, 150 feet

Photo Tip: The side views are made difficult by obstructions but there are excellent 3/4 views.

Notes: There is new coverings on the sides and part of the portals which gives it a great appearance in this natural setting. In 1936 it was washed off its abutments and after returning it, cables were installed to anchor it and these are still present. In 1982 the roof collapsed from a heavy snow load and it was repaired the same year.

World Index Number: 29-05-11

National Register of Historic Places: Not listed

Clark Covered Bridge
(Pinsley Railroad Covered Bridge)

Township: Lincoln
County: Grafton County
GPS Position: N 44° 02.994' W 71° 41.273'
Directions: from the town of North Woodstock go north on US-3/Daniel Webster Highway/Main St. for 1.1 miles to Clark's Trading Post. The bridge is on their grounds and there is an admission charge. However you can view and photograph the bridge from near the parking lot. Walk from the parking lot area farthest from the gift shop and you will soon see it.
Crosses: Pemigewasset River
Carries: Interior rail

Builder: Unknown
Year Built: 1904 (M1965)
Truss Type: Howe
Dimensions: 1 Span, 120 feet

Photo Tip: You cannot walk into or through the bridge but there is a great 3/4 view.

Notes: This railroad bridge was originally located in Vermont between Barre and Montpelier. The owners of the Clark's Trading Post attraction acquired it from its abandoned position, moved it and rebuilt it in its present position in 1965. It is used in conjunction with a steam engine from the White Mountain Rail Line.

World Index Number: 29-05-14 Formerly 45-12-16

National Register of Historic Places: Not listed

Jack O'Lantern Resort Covered Bridge

Township: Woodstock
County: Grafton County
GPS Position: N 43° 56.982' W 71° 40.746'
Directions: From the town of Compton go north on NH-175 for 3.8 miles and turn left on Cross Road. After 0.7 miles turn right on US-3/Daniel Webster Highway and proceed 2.5 miles to the Jack O'Lantern Resort. Although it is on private property, you can see and photograph it from the parking lot.

Crosses: Pond
Carries: None

Builder: Milton Graton
Year Built: 1986
Truss Type: Town

Dimensions: 1 Span, 79 feet

Photo Tip: Although found on a private golf course, you can photograph it from the parking lot. Go to the area farthest from the building and look to the right side. A longer lens is helpful, perhaps about 200 mm.

Notes: This bridge is a replica of the Woodstock Covered bridge which was destroyed by fire in 1971. It was built to half the size of the original and was completed by Milton Graton and then brought by train to the site.

World Index Number: 29-05-18

National Register of Historic Places: Not listed

Packard Hill Covered Bridge

Township: Lebanon
County: Grafton County
GPS Position: N 43° 38.298' W 72° 13.298'
Directions: From the town of Lebanon go east on Bank St/US-4 for 0.6 miles and turn left to continue on the Bank Street Extension for another 0.9 miles, then turn right onto Riverside Drive where the bridge is located.

Crosses: Mascoma River
Carries: Riverside Drive

Builder: Arnold Graton Associates
Year Built: 1991
Truss Type: Town
Dimensions: 1 Span, 76 feet

Photo Tip: The sides are obstructed but the portal view is excellent with the bridge book ended by the pedestrian walkway and a line of trees.

Notes: This bridge is a replica of the original covered bridge that was built in this spot in 1878 and removed in in 1952. Between 1952 and 1991 a Bailey Bridge carried the traffic.

World Index Number: 29-05-50#2

National Register of Historic Places: Not listed

Squam River Covered Bridge

Township: Ashland
County: Grafton County
GPS Position: N 43° 43.092' W 71° 37.114'
Directions: From the town of Holderness go southwest on NH-25/US-3/Daniel Webster Highway for 1.8 miles and turn right on River Road where you will reach the bridge shortly.

Crosses: Squam Lake
Carries: River Road

Builder: Milton Graton and Sons
Year Built: 1990
Truss Type: Town
Dimensions: 1 Span, 61 feet
Photo Tip: There is a good side view from the beach.

Notes: This bridge came into existence because the people of the town of Ashland wanted it instead of a concrete and steel bridge that was being planned by the state. It is a one lane bridge which has a decided camber designed in.

World Index Number: 29-05-112

National Register of Historic Places: Not listed

Hillsborough County

Greenfield-Hancock Covered Bridge
(County Covered Bridge)

Township: Greenfield-Hancock
County: Hillsborough County
GPS Position: N 42° 57.389' W 71° 56.069'
Directions: From the town of Hancock go east on Norway Hill Road, continuing on Duncan Road and Forest Road and after 2.5 miles you will reach the bridge.

Crosses: Contookook River
Carries: Forest Road

Builder: Henry Pratt
Year Built: 1937 (R1981) (R2001)
Truss Type: Pratt
Dimensions: 1 Span, 87 feet

Photo Tip: There is a good side view that can be reached from the SW corner.

Notes: The township line between Greenfield and Hancock falls in the center of the bridge as a sign shows. This bridge is a replacement of an 1852 bridge that was destroyed in a flood in 1936.

World Index Number: 29-06-02#2

National Register of Historic Places: Not listed

Blood Brook Covered Bridge

Township: Wilton
County: Hillsborough County
GPS Position: N 42° 49.766' W 71° 46.705'
Directions: From the town of Wilton go southwest on Island St. and shortly turn right on NH-101/NH-31 and proceed for 3.4 miles and turn right on Russell Hill Road and then shortly make a sharp right back toward NH-31 and the bridge is a short distance at the end of the road..

Crosses: Blood Brook
Carries: Abandoned road

Builder: Unknown
Year Built: 1930s
Truss Type: Town Boxed Pony
Dimensions: 1 Span, 52 feet

Photo Tip: Easy from all sides. Look for the information sign on the end of one side.

Notes: This is one of three Boxed Pony bridges in New Hampshire. They have covered sides and no top. Since they are listed in the "World Guide to Covered Bridges", we also list them.

World Index Number: 29-06-P1

National Register of Historic Places: Not listed

Merrimack County

Cileyville Covered Bridge
(Bog Covered Bridge)

Township: Andover
County: Merrimack County
GPS Position: N 43° 25.855' W 71° 52.081'
Directions: From the town of Andover go west on NH-11/Main St for 2.4 miles where you will see the bridge.

Crosses: Blackwater River
Carries: NH-11

Builder: Print Atwood, Al Emerson and Charles Wilson
Year Built: 1887 (R1962) (R1982) (R2003)
Truss Type: Town
Dimensions: 1 Span, 53 feet

Photo Tip: This is a beautiful bridge and the large flag on the side will provide excellent images.

Notes: Originally called the Bog Covered Bridge, it was rebuilt in 2003. The large U.S flag on the side sets it off beautifully.

World Index Number: 29-07-01

National Register of Historic Places: 3/16/1989

Keniston Covered Bridge

Township: Andover
County: Merrimack County
GPS Position: N 43° 26.089' W 71° 50.177'
Directions: From the town of Andover go west on NH-11/US-4/Main St. for 0.4 miles and turn left on Bridge St. where you will find the bridge in 0.1 miles.

Crosses: Blackwater River
Carries: Bridge St.

Builder: Albert Hamilton
Year Built: 1882 (R1949) (R1972) (R1981) (R2003)
Truss Type: Town
Dimensions:1 Span, 62 feet

Photo Tip: There are excellent views from all sides especially a 3/4 view showing the open town trusses.

Notes: This bridge is unusual in that it has almost no sideboards and the town trusses are well shown.

World Index Number: 29-07-02

National Register of Historic Places: 3/16/1989

Bement Covered Bridge

Township: Bradford
County: Merrimack County
GPS Position: N 43° 15.872' W 71° 57.161'
Directions: In the town of Bradford go south on Center Road off NH-103 for a short distance and you will find the bridge.

Crosses: West Branch of the Warner River
Carries: Center Road

Builder: Stephen H. Long

Year Built: 1854 (R1947) (R1969) (R1987) (R1990)
Truss Type: Long
Dimensions: 1 Span, 61 feet

Photo Tip: Side views are obstructed but there is a good 3/4 view from the east side.

Notes: The builder, Stephen Long, used the Long truss system for this bridge which was a support system which he patented. The 1987 repairs were necessitated by a vehicle damaging it.

World Index Number: 29-07-03

National Register of Historic Places: 11/21/1976

Waterloo Station Covered Bridge

Township: Warner
County: Merrimack County
GPS Position: N 43° 17.302' W 71° 51.353'
Directions: From the town of Bradford go southeast on NH-103 for 6.3 miles and turn right on Newmarket Road and you will find the bridge in 0.2 miles.

Crosses: Warner River
Carries: Newmarket Road

Builder: Dutton Woods
Year Built: 1857 (R1970) (R1987)
Truss Type: Town
Dimensions: 1 Span, 76 feet

Photo Tip: There is a good 3/4 view down near water level.

Notes: This bridge is unpainted and the weathered texture and natural setting look very good, especially set off by the red roof.

World Index Number: 29-07-04

National Register of Historic Places: 11/21/1976

Dalton Covered Bridge
(Joppa Road Bridge)

Township: Warner
County: Merrimack County
GPS Position: N 43° 16.631' W 71° 48.671'
Directions: From the town of Bradford go east on NH-103 for 8.0 miles and turn right on Joppa Hill Road where the bridge is found in 0.2 miles

Crosses: Warner River
Carries: Joppa Hill Road

Builder: Joshua Sanborn
Year Built: 1853 (R1871) (R1964) (R1990)
Truss Type: Long and Queen

Dimensions: 1 Span, 77 feet

Photo Tip: There is an easy and excellent side view of this weathered bridge.

Notes: This bridge has an interesting truss system, a combination of the Long truss with Queenpost, although it has been wrongly described as a Kingpost and Queenpost in some sources.

World Index Number: 29-07-05

National Register of Historic Places: 11/21/1976

Contoocook Railroad Covered Bridge

Township: Hopkinton
County: Merrimack County
GPS Position: N 43° 13.375' W 71° 42.833'

Directions: In the town of Contoocook the bridge is by Main St. where it crosses the Contoocook River.

Crosses: Contoocook River
Carries: Main St. (Bypassed Section)

Builder: David Hazelton for the Boston & Maine Railroad.
Year Built: 1889
Truss Type: Double Town
Dimensions: 2 Span, 157 feet

Photo Tip: Easy views from front and sides and you can also photograph the interior.

Notes: This is the oldest surviving railroad covered bridge. It has had an interesting career, having washed off its abutments in 1936 and 1938, and from 1962 till 1990 it was used as a merchant's warehouse.

World Index Number: 29-07-07#2

National Register of Historic Places: 3/16/2006

Rowell Covered Bridge

Township: Hopkinton
County: Merrimack County
GPS Position: N 43° 11.539' W 71° 44.902'
Directions: From the town of Contoocook go south on NH-127/Maple Street for 3.4 miles and turn left on Clement Hill Road where you will see the bridge.

Crosses: Contoocook River
Carries: Clement Hill Road

Builder: Horace, Enoch and Warren Childs
Year Built: 1853 (R1930) (R1965) (R1982) (R1995)
Truss Type: Long and Burr Arch
Dimensions: 1 Span (Center pier added), 167 feet

Photo Tip: With care when water levels are not high, you can go onto the rocks on the downstream side for an excellent side view.

Notes: Have a look at the interesting truss system, Long trusses sandwiching a Burr Arch. This bridge has a history of instability, in its early days vibrations of cattle moving through it shook it off its abutments and in 1930 a center pier was added. The sides are open in the top half and the roof has a large overhang.

World Index Number: 29-07-08

National Register of Historic Places: 11/21/1976

Sulphite Railroad Covered Bridge

Township: Franklin
County: Merrimack County
GPS Position: N 43° 26.708' W 71° 38.119'
Directions: In the town of Franklin go east on NH-11/US-3/Central St from the junction at NH-127 after 0.9 miles you will see the bridge crossing the Winnipesaukee River. At the east side before the bridge there is access to the Winnipesaukee River Trail and the bridge is 0.5 miles along the trail.

Crosses: Winnipesaukee River
Carries: Winnipesaukee River Trail

Builder: Boston and Maine Railroad
Year Built: 1896
Truss Type: Pratt
Dimensions: 3 Spans, 180 feet

Photo Tip: There is a good view from the side as you approach on the trail. Don't venture onto the bridge.

Notes: This has often been called the "upside down" bridge because the rail tracks were on top of what would be considered the roof of the bridge. The bridge was destroyed in a fire in 1980 and the cost of replacing it was estimated at $500,000 which probably means it won't happen. It is not safe to walk across the bridge.

World Index Number: 29-07-09

National Register of Historic Places: 6/11/1975

New England College Covered Bridge

Township: Henniker
County: Merrimack County

GPS Position: N 43° 10.646' W 71° 49.338'
Directions: Found in the town of Henniker on the New England College Campus off of US-202

Crosses: Contoocook River
Carries: Interior Road

Builder: Milton and Arnold Graton
Year Built: 1972
Truss Type: Town
Dimensions: 1 Span, 137 feet

Photo Tip: Excellent images from front and interesting look from interior including one with the trusses framing a stone arch bridge upstream.

Notes: The Gratons built this bridge in a completely authentic manner including moving it into place using a system of pulleys and a team of oxen.

World Index Number: 29-07-12

National Register of Historic Places: Not listed

Stratford County

Rollins Farm Covered Bridge
(Clement Road Ext. Covered Bridge)

Township: Rollinsford
County: Stratford County
GPS Position: N 43° 13.38' W 70° 51.12'
Directions: From the town of Dover go northeast on Broadway and continue on Rollins Road to the intersection of Clement Road, a total of about 2.1 miles. walk 0.3 miles east, opposite Clements Road where you will reach the bridge.

Crosses: Boston and Maine Railroad
Carries: Old Path

Builder: Boston & Maine Railroad
Year Built: 1904
Truss Type: Boxed Pony Queen
Dimensions: 1 Span, 43 feet

Photo Tip: Good views from the front and the graffiti and wear may add to the image.

Notes: This boxed pony bridge was built to cross the Boston and Maine Railroad but lies in disrepair. It is included in the "World Guide to Covered bridges" and we have therefore included it.

World Index Number: 29-09-P1

National Register of Historic Places: Not listed

Sullivan County
Blacksmith Shop Covered Bridge

Township: Cornish
County: Sullivan County
GPS Position: N 43° 27.770' W 72° 21.237'
Directions: from the town of Windsor take Town House Road off NH-12A and the bridge is 1.9 miles.

Crosses: Mill Brook
Carries: Town House Road

Builder: James Tasker
Year Built: 1881 (R1993)
Truss Type: Multiple Kingpost
Dimensions: 1 Span, 96 feet

Photo Tip: Easy from all sides including a brook level side view.

Notes: The bridge was repaired by Milton Graton in 1983 and it was re-opened for pedestrian traffic only. It is unpainted and the weathered texture looks excellent, especially in the snow.

World Index Number: 29-10-01

National Register of Historic Places: Not listed

Dingleton Covered Bridge

Township: Cornish
County: Sullivan County
GPS Position: N 43° 27.868' W 72° 22.151'
Directions: In the village of Cornish look for the bridge on Root Hill Rd. just south of the intersection with Town House Road.

Crosses: Mill Brook
Carries: Root Hill Rd.

Builder: James Tasker
Year Built: 1882 (R1983)
Truss Type: Multiple Kingpost
Dimensions: 1 Span, 78 feet

Photo Tip: Good from all sides and an exceptional side view showing the bridge perched on tall abutments.

Notes: An unpainted bridge in a quiet river valley, the top half of the sides is open revealing the trusses. The 1983 repairs were done by Milton Graton.
World Index Number: 29-10-02

National Register of Historic Places: 11/8/1978

Pier Railroad Covered Bridge
(Chandler Station Covered Bridge)

Township: Newport
County: Sullivan County
GPS Position: N 43° 21.721' W 72° 14.520'
Directions: From the town of go west on NH-103/NH-11/John Stark Highway for 2.1 miles and turn left on Chandlers Mill Road. The bridge is found in 1.4 miles.
Crosses: Sugar River
Carries: Chandlers Mill Road

Builder: Boston and Maine Railroad
Year Built: 1896 (R1909)
Truss Type: Double Town

Dimensions: 2 Span, 228 feet

Photo Tip: Excellent locations from the front and if you go back to the edge of the road, you can get an impressive side view. I took three digital images and joined them in a panorama.

Notes: This is an impressive bridge, very heavily built with a large double town truss system so that it could bear the weight of heavy trains. The rails have been removed and the interior now has a plank floor.

World Index Number: 29-10-03#2

National Register of Historic Places: 6/10/1975

Wright Railroad Covered Bridge

Township: Newport
County: Sullivan County
GPS Position: N 43° 21.533' W 72° 15.517'

Directions: from the town of Newport go west on NH-103/NH-11/John Stark Highway for 2.4 miles and turn left on Chandlers Mill Road. After 0.2 miles you will see a small parking lot where there is access to the abandoned railway right-of-way. Follow it for 0.4 miles to reach the bridge. You can see the bridge from the lot.

Crosses: Sugar River
Carries: Railway right-of-way

Builder: Boston and Maine Railroad
Year Built: 1895 (R1906)
Truss Type: Double Town with Burr Arch
Dimensions: 1 Span, 124 feet

Builder: Boston and Maine Railroad
Year Built: 1895 (R1906)
Truss Type: Double Town with Burr Arch
Dimensions: 1 Span, 124 feet

Photo Tip: There are beautiful portal images available and consider also the massive truss structure in the interior.

Notes: The weight of the trains needed a substantial structure and this bridge has a massive burr arch sandwiched between two heavy Town trusses. The bridge looks to be in good shape.

World Index Number: 29-10-04#2

National Register of Historic Places: 6/10/1975

Corbin Covered Bridge

Township: Newport
County: Sullivan County

GPS Position: N 43° 23.456' W 72° 11.699'

Directions: From the town of Newport go north on Main St for 0.9 miles and turn left on Corbin Rd where you will find the bridge in 1.5 miles.

Crosses: Sugar River

Carries: Corbin Rd

Builder: Arnold Graton and Associates
Year Built: 1994 (Rebuild of 1845 bridge)
Truss Type: Town
Dimensions: 1 Span, 102 feet

Photo Tip: Easy from all sides but especially side views from river level.

Notes: The original covered bridge was built in 1845 by an unknown builder and it was destroyed by arson in 1993. An authentic rebuild was completed in 1994 even including the use of oxen for transport. The builder Arnold Graton is famous for his meticulous work as was his father Milton Graton. The bridge is without windows like most early bridges and in a quiet country setting.

World Index Number: 29-10-05#2

National Register of Historic Places: Not listed

McDermott Covered Bridge

Township: Langdon
County: Sullivan County
GPS Position: N 43° 10.206' W 72° 20.744'
Directions: From the town of South Acworth go southwest on NH-123A for 3.7 miles and turn right on Crane Brook Road where the bridge is a short distance.

Crosses: Cold River
Carries: Crane Brook Road (Bypassed)

Builder: Albert S. Granger
Year Built: 1869 (R1961)
Truss Type: Town with Arch
Dimensions: 1 Span, 86 feet
Photo Tip: With careful placement near the highway's edge you can get a good 3/4 view

Notes: This unpainted structure is well weathered but seems in reasonable shape. It was bypassed in 1964.

World Index Number: 29-10-06

National Register of Historic Places: Not listed

Prentiss Covered Bridge
(Drewsville Covered Bridge)

Township: Langdon
County: Sullivan County
GPS Position: N 43° 09.236' W 72° 23.611'
Directions: From the town of Langdon head west on Village Road and continue on Langdon Road, Lower Cemetery Road and Cheshire Turnpike, in total about 2.0 miles, where you will find the bridge.

Crosses: Great Brook
Carries: Cheshire Turnpike (Bypassed)

Builder: Albert S. Granger
Year Built: 1869 (R2000)

Truss Type: Town
Dimensions: 1 Span, 35 feet

Photo Tip: There is a good side view from the highway beside it but be careful of traffic.
Notes: This is New Hampshire's smallest Covered Bridge. It was bypassed in 1954.

World Index Number: 29-10-07

National Register of Historic Places: 5/24/1973

Meriden Covered Bridge
(Mill Covered Bridge)

Township: Plainfield
County: Sullivan County
GPS Position: N 43° 33.197' W 72° 15.922'
Directions: From the town of Meriden go 0.9 miles northwest on Main St. and turn left on Colby Hill Road where you will see the bridge.

Crosses: Blood's Brook
Carries: Colby Hill Road

Builder: James Tasker
Year Built: 1880 (R1954) (R1963) (R1977) (R1985)
Truss Type: Multiple Kingpost
Dimensions: 1+ Span, 80 feet

Photo Tip: Sides views can be difficult and obstructed, with 3/4 views perhaps the best.

Notes: This bridge has suffered through calamities, Hurricane Carol damaged it in 1954 and it was probably then that a steel pier was added. It also experienced heavy snows in 1977 which caused the roof to collapse. It is unpainted and open on half of the sides.

World Index Number: 29-10-08

National Register of Historic Places: 8/27/1980

Blow-Me-Down Covered Bridge
(Bayliss Covered Bridge)

Township: Cornish
County: Sullivan County
GPS Position: N 43° 31.026' W 72° 22.439'
Directions: from the town of Plainfield go southwest on NH-12A for 1.0 mile and turn left on Thrasher Rd and continue onto Platt Rd. In 0.5 miles turn right onto Lang Rd. where you will see the bridge.

Crosses: Blow-Me-Down Brook
Carries: Lang Rd.

Builder: James Tasker
Year Built: C1860 (R1980) (R2002)
Truss Type: Multiple Kingpost
Dimensions: 1 Span, 86 feet

Photo Tip: There may be a good side view which would include the waterfall but my visit in winter conditions made that too dangerous. It is in a quiet natural setting.

Notes: The bridge was repaired by Milton and Arnold Graton in 1980. It is unpainted and has a natural rustic appearance.

World Index Number: 29-10-10

National Register of Historic Places: 3/2/2001

Sullivan County and Windsor County, Vermont

Windsor-Cornish Covered Bridge

Township: Windsor (Vermont) Cornish (New Hampshire)
County: Windsor (Vermont) Sullivan (New Hampshire)

GPS Position: N 43° 28.375' W 72° 22.996'
Directions: From the town of Windsor, Vermont, take US-5/ VT-12/ Main St. south for 0.3 miles and turn left on Bridge St. From the town of Cornish, New Hampshire, take Mill Village Road and continue on Town House Road and NH-12 for 1.5 miles and the bridge will appear on your left.

Crosses: Connecticut River
Carries: Bridge Street (Vermont) Cornish Toll Road (New Hampshire)

Builder: James Tasker & Bela J. Fletcher
Year Built: 1866 (R1887) (R1892)(R1887) (R1925) (R1887) (R1938) (R1955) (R1977) (R1989) (R2001)
Truss Type: Town
Dimensions: 2 Span, 449 Feet, 2 Lanes
Photo Tip: There are good views from front and sides but watch for traffic. The new Hampshire side is a bit better

Notes: This is one of the finest covered bridges in North America with a toe in Vermont and the bulk in New Hampshire. It is the longest two span bridge in the world.

World Index Number: 45-14-14#2 (Vermont) 29-10-09#2 (New Hampshire)

National **Register of Historic Places**: November 21. 1976

Self Guided Tours

Carroll County 7 Bridges - 2 hours driving

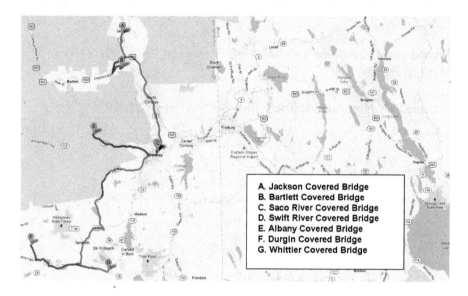

A. Jackson Covered Bridge
B. Bartlett Covered Bridge
C. Saco River Covered Bridge
D. Swift River Covered Bridge
E. Albany Covered Bridge
F. Durgin Covered Bridge
G. Whittier Covered Bridge

We start our tour at the **Jackson Covered Bridge** which is at GPS position N 44° 08.499' W 71° 11.208'.

In the town of Jackson take NH-16A/Mains St./Village Rd. east from the junction of NH-16 for 400 feet where you will see the bridge.

Our next stop is the **Bartlett Covered Bridge** which is at GPS coordinates N 44° 05.675' W 71° 11.208'.

Head northwest on NH-16 N/Pinkham Notch Rd and shortly take a sharp left onto NH-16 S/Pinkham Notch Rd and drive for 2.3 miles and turn right onto US-302 W/Crawford Notch Rd/Main St. In 2.1 miles turn left onto West Side Rd and after another 1.1 miles turn right on an unnamed road and the bridge is found in 0.5 miles. (6.1 miles – about 13 minutes)

Now we head for the Saco River Covered Bridge which is at GPS position N 43° 58.992' W 71° 06.983'.

Head west for 0.5 miles and turn left onto West Side Rd and drive another 1.1 miles. Turn right onto US-302 E/Crawford Notch Rd and proceed for 10.3 miles. Continue onto NH-16 S/White Mountain Hwy for 2.1 miles and make a slight right onto East Side Rd where you will find the bridge in 0.5 miles. (14.5 miles – about 25 minutes)

We will now head for the **Swift River Covered Bridge** which is found at GPS coordinates N 43° 59.066' W 71° 07.175'.

Head southwest on East Side Rd and after 0.1 miles turn right onto West Side Rd and you will see the bridge in 0.1 miles. (0.3 miles – about 1 minute)

Our next destination is the **Albany Covered Bridge** found at GPS position N 44° 00.342' W 71° 14.473'.

Head south on West Side Rd toward Hillside Ave, continuing onto Washington Stand after 0.4 miles turn right onto Main St. Proceed for 0.8 miles and turn right onto NH-112 W/Kancamagus Hwy and then after 6.2 miles turn right onto Passaconaway Rd where the bridge is a short distance. (7.5 miles – about 13 minutes)

Now we head for **Durgin Covered Bridge** which is at GPS coordinates N 43° 51.340' W 71° 21.866'.

Head northwest on Passaconaway Rd toward NH-112 E/Kancamagus Hwy and shortly turn left onto NH-112 E/Kancamagus Hwy and continue for 6.2 miles where you turn right onto NH-16 S/White Mountain Hwy. In 11.0 miles turn right onto NH-113 W/Deer Hill/Silver Lake Rd and shortly take the 1st right onto NH-113 W/Chocorua Rd. In 2.9 miles turn left onto NH-113 W/Chocorua Rd/Tamworth Rd and then in 2.0 miles turn right onto NH-113 W/Whittier Rd. Drive another 0.4 miles and turn right onto NH-113 W/NH-25 W/Bearcamp Hwy and then proceed for 2.8 miles and turn right onto NH-113 W/Jackman Pond Rd. In 1.7 miles turn right onto Foss Flats Rd and the bridge is 1.5 miles. (28.7 miles – about 48 minutes)

Our last stop is the **Whittier Covered Bridge** whose GPS position is N 43° 49.287' W 71° 12.738'.

Head southeast on Foss Flats Rd toward Cold River Rd and in 1.5 miles turn left onto NH-113 E/Beede Flats Rd. After 1.7 miles turn left onto NH-113 E/NH-25 E/Whittier Rd and continue for 5.9 miles. Turn left onto Nudd Rd and the bridge is a short distance. (9.2 miles – about 19 minutes)

Self Guided Tours
Cheshire County Tour - 6 Bridges, 40 minutes driving

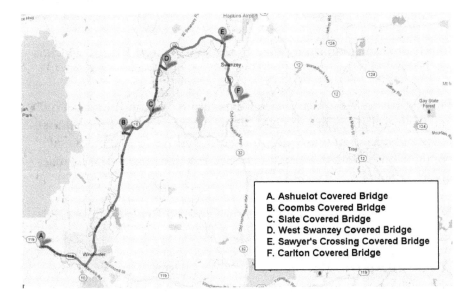

> A. Ashuelot Covered Bridge
> B. Coombs Covered Bridge
> C. Slate Covered Bridge
> D. West Swanzey Covered Bridge
> E. Sawyer's Crossing Covered Bridge
> F. Carlton Covered Bridge

Our tour begins at one of the finest covered bridges, the **Ashuelot Covered Bridge.** It GPS position is N 42° 46.644' W 72° 25.408'.

The Ashuelot Covered Bridge is found close to the town of Winchester, head west on NH-119/Hinsdale from the town and turn left on Gunn Mountain Road where you will see the bridge.

Our second stop is the **Coombs Covered Bridge** whose GPS coordinates are N 42° 50.281' W 72° 21.649'.

Head north on Gunn Mountain Rd toward NH-119 E/Hinsdale Rd and shortly turn right onto NH-119 E/Hinsdale Rd After 1.9 miles turn left onto NH-10 N/NH-119 E/Main St and proceed for 5.4 miles where you turn left onto Coombs Bridge Rd. The bridge is found after 0.3 miles (7.6 miles – about 14 minutes)

Next we will head for **Slate Covered Bridge** whose GPS position is N 42° 50.855' W 72° 20.411'.

Head northeast on Coombs Bridge Rd toward Roberts Ln and after 0.3 miles turn left onto NH-10 N/Keene Rd. In another 0.3 miles turn right onto Westport Village Rd and you will see the bridge in 0.9 miles (1.4 miles – about 4 minutes)

Our next destination is the **West Swanzey Covered Bridge** which is at GPS coordinates N 42° 52.303' W 72° 19.688'.

Head north on Westport Village Rd toward Kempton Rd for 0.4 miles and make a slight right onto NH-10 N/W Swanzey Rd. Proceed for 1.5 miles and turn right onto California St, then drive for 0.2 miles and continue onto Main St where the bridge is a short distance. (2.2 miles – about 5 minutes)

Now we head for **Sawyer's Crossing Covered Bridge** whose GPS coordinates are N 42° 53.176' W 72° 17.173'.

Head northwest on Main St toward N Winchester St and continue onto California St. After 0.2 miles turn right onto NH-10 N/W Swanzey Rd and after 0.9 miles make a slight right onto Sawyers Crossing Rd. In 1.5 miles turn right to stay on Sawyers Crossing Rd and the bridge is 0.6 miles. (3.3 miles – about 8 minutes)

Our final stop is the **Carlton Covered Bridge** which is at GPS position N 42° 51.277' W 72° 16.453'.

Head east on Sawyers Crossing Rd and after 0.1 miles turn right to stay on Sawyers Crossing Rd. Proceed for 0.9 miles and continue onto NH-32 S/Old Homestead Hwy for another 1.4 miles. Turn left onto Carlton Rd and the bridge is 0.2 miles. (2.6 miles– about 7 minutes)

Self-Guided Tour
Coős County Tour- 6 Bridges- 40 minutes driving

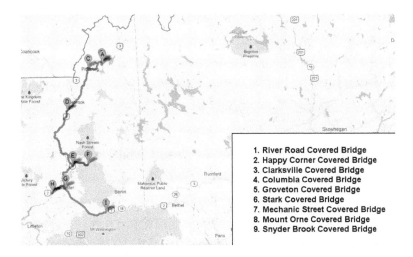

1. River Road Covered Bridge
2. Happy Corner Covered Bridge
3. Clarksville Covered Bridge
4. Columbia Covered Bridge
5. Groveton Covered Bridge
6. Stark Covered Bridge
7. Mechanic Street Covered Bridge
8. Mount Orne Covered Bridge
9. Snyder Brook Covered Bridge

Our first stop is **River Road Covered Bridge** which is at GPS position N 45° 04.355' W 71° 18.340'. From the town of Pittsburg go east on US-3/Daniel Webster Highway for 5.9 miles and turn right on River Road where the bridge is found in 1.2 miles.

From here we will head to **Happy Corner Covered Bridge** found at GPS coordinates N 45° 05.043' W 71° 18.814'.

Head southwest on River Rd toward Philbrook Rd and shortly take the 1st right onto Philbrook Rd. In 0.4 miles take the 2nd right onto Glenwood Dr and then in 0.8 miles turn right onto Hill-Danforth Rd and you will find the bridge. (1.4 miles – about 6 minutes)

Now we proceed to the **Clarksville Covered Bridge** which is at GPS position N 45° 03.280' W 71° 24.410'.

Head north on Hill-Danforth Rd toward US-3 S/Daniel Webster Hwy and after 0.2 miles turn left onto US-3 S/Daniel Webster Hwy and continue to follow US-3 S for 6.5 miles where you turn left onto Bacon Rd and find the bridge. (6.7 miles – about 11 minutes)

Our next stop is the **Columbia Covered Bridge** which is at the border with Vermont and it is at GPS position N 44° 51.159' W 71° 33.050'.

Head north on Bacon Rd toward US-3 S and shortly turn right onto US-3 N and proceed for 0.9 miles where you will take the 1st right onto NH-145 S/Mill St, and continue to follow NH-145 S for 13.1 miles. Turn left onto US-3 S/Daniel Webster Hwy/Main St and Columbia Bridge Rd is 4.2 miles where you will find the bridge. (18.3 miles – about 28 minutes)

We now head for **Groveton Covered Bridge** which is at GPS coordinates N 44° 35.749' W 71° 30.684'.

Head southwest on US-3 S/Daniel Webster Hwy toward Columbia Bridge Rd and after 8.9 miles turn right onto VT-105 W, entering Vermont. In 0.2 miles take the 2nd left onto VT-102 S and drive for 8.9 miles where you turn left onto Lamoureux Rd. Proceed for 0.6 miles and continue onto Maidstone Bridge Rd as you re-enter New Hampshire and in 0.2 miles turn right onto US-3 S/Daniel Webster Hwy. Drive for 4.7 miles and make a slight right onto Church St/State St and after 0.2 miles continue onto Main St. In a short distance you will see the bridge on a bypassed section. (23.7 miles – about 41 minutes)

The next stop is the **Stark Covered Bridge** which is found at GPS position N 44° 36.043' W 71° 24.464'.

Head east toward NH-110 W/Berlin-Groveton Hwy and shortly turn left onto NH-110 E/Berlin-Groveton Hwy and after 6.7 miles turn left onto Northside Rd where you will find the bridge. (6.8 miles – about 10 minutes)

Now we head for **Mechanic Street Covered Bridge** found at GPS coordinates N 44° 29.194' W 71° 33.869'.

Head southeast on Northside Rd toward NH-110 E/Stark Hwy and turn right onto NH-110 W/Stark Hwy. After 6.8 miles turn left onto US-3 S/Main St and proceed for 9.8 miles where you turn left onto

Mechanic St where the bridge is found ln 0.3 miles. (16.8 miles – about 28 minutes)

From here we head back towards the Vermont border and the **Mount Orne Covered Bridge** which is at GPS position N 44° 27.634' W 71° 39.206'.

Head north on Pleasant St toward Mechanic St and turn left onto Mechanic St and drive 0.3 miles where you turn right onto US-2 W/Main St, entering Vermont. In 5.7 miles make a slight left onto River Rd and you will find the bridge in 0.4 miles. (6.3 miles – about 12 minutes)

Our last stop is the **Snyder Brook Covered Bridge** which is a boxed pony with covered sides but no roof. It is found at GPS position N 44° 22.290' W 71° 17.332'.

Head north on River Rd toward US-2 W and after 0.4 miles continue onto US-2 E , entering New Hampshire. Proceed for 5.7 miles and make a slight left onto US-2 E/Portland St. Continue to follow US-2 E for 17.8 miles where you will see the parking lot for the national Forest. The bridge is found 0.2 miles on the old railroad right of way. from the information sign, a few steps will bring you to the rail right of way and you should go to the left. (23.9 miles – about 30 minutes)

This is the last stop on our tour

Self Guided Tours

Grafton County Tour 12 Bridges - 3 hour 30 minutes driving

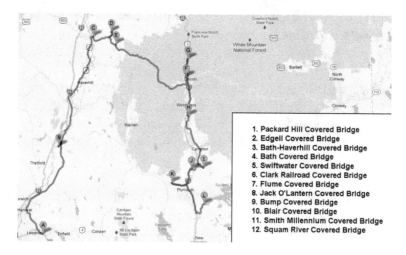

1. Packard Hill Covered Bridge
2. Edgell Covered Bridge
3. Bath-Haverhill Covered Bridge
4. Bath Covered Bridge
5. Swiftwater Covered Bridge
6. Clark Railroad Covered Bridge
7. Flume Covered Bridge
8. Jack O'Lantern Covered Bridge
9. Bump Covered Bridge
10. Blair Covered Bridge
11. Smith Millennium Covered Bridge
12. Squam River Covered Bridge

We start our tour at the **Packard Hill Covered Bridge** which is at GPS position N 43° 38.298' W 72° 13.298'.

From the town of Lebanon go east on Bank St/US-4 for 0.6 miles and turn left to continue on the Bank Street Extension for another 0.9 miles, then turn right onto Riverside Drive where the bridge is located.

Our next stop is the **Edgell Covered Bridge** which is at GPS coordinates N 43° 52.055' W 72° 09.903'.

Head west on Riverside Dr toward Bank Street Extension and shortly turn left onto Bank Street Extension and after 0.6 miles turn right onto Alden Rd/Heater Rd and drive for 0.9 miles. Turn right onto Route 120 N and drive 4.7 miles, then turn right onto Lyme Rd and proceed for a further 0.9 miles. At the traffic circle, continue straight onto NH-10 N/Lyme Rd and continue to follow NH-10 N for 9.1 miles where you turn right onto NH-10 N/Main St. Continue to follow NH-10 N for 5.3 miles where you turn left onto River Rd and the bridge site is 1.0 mile. (22.5 miles – about 39 minutes)

We now head for **Bath-Haverhill Covered Bridge** which is found at GPS position N 44° 09.252' W 72° 02.165'.

Head northeast on River Rd and after 1.0 mile turn left onto NH-10 N/Orford Rd and continue for 2.0 miles. Turn left onto New Hampshire 25A W/Bridge St and continue to follow Bridge St, entering Vermont. In 0.3 miles turn right onto U.S. Route 5 N/Main St and follow it for 19.2 miles, where you re-enter new Hampshire. After 0.5 miles turn left onto Monroe Rd and shortly take the 1st right onto Oak Hill St and then left onto N Court St where you will see the bridge. (23.2 miles – about 33 minutes)

Next we will head for one of the finest covered bridges in North America, the **Bath Covered Bridge**. it is at GPS position N 44° 10.007' W 71° 58.084'

Head southeast on N Court St toward Ammonoosuc St and shortly take the 1st right onto Oak Hill St and then continue onto Railroad St for 0.1 miles where you turn right toward Central St and immediately after take the 1st left onto Central St. Drive 0.9 miles and turn left onto NH-10 N/US-302 E/Dartmouth College Hwy and proceed for 3.8 miles. Make a sharp left onto W Bath Rd where you will cross the bridge. There is good parking on the far side. (5.1 miles – about 10 minutes)

Our next site is the **Swiftwater Covered Bridge** which is found at GPS position N 44° 08.074' W 71° 57.038'.

Head back across Bath Rd and make a sharp right onto NH-10 S/US-302 W/Lisbon Rd and then after 1.3 miles turn left onto NH-112 E/Wild Ammonoosuc Rd. Proceed for 2.1 miles and turn left onto Porter Rd and you will see the bridge in 0.1 miles. (3.7 miles – about 7 minutes)

Now we head for **Clark Railroad Covered Bridge** which is at GPS coordinates N 44° 02.994' W 71° 41.273'.

Head east on Porter Rd and after 0.1 miles make a slight left onto NH-112 E/Wild Ammonoosuc Rd where you drive for 18.3

miles. Turn left onto US-3 N/Daniel Webster Hwy/Main St and after 1.4 miles you will see the Clark's Trading Post Attraction.
The bridge is on their grounds and there is an admission charge. However you can view and photograph the bridge from near the parking lot. Walk from the parking lot area farthest from the gift shop and you will soon see it. (19.8 miles – about 31 minutes)

Next we head for the **Flume Covered Bridge** which is Flume Reservation area of the Franconia State Park and is at GPS position N 44° 05.956' W 71° 40.599'. Note there is an admission charge.

Head northwest on US-3 N/Daniel Webster Hwy toward Red House Way and after 3.3 miles turn right and the parking lot of the Flume Gorge is 0.2 miles. (3.5 miles – about 6 minutes)

Now we will go to **Jack O'Lantern Covered Bridge** which is found at GPS coordinates N 43° 56.982' W 71° 40.746'.

Head back to US-3 and turn left and after 2.4 miles turn right to merge onto I-93 S toward Concord. Drive 7.7 miles and take exit 30 to merge onto US-3 S/Daniel Webster Hwy toward Thornton. In 1.1 miles turn left onto Hillside Dr and you will see the resort. You can see the bridge from the lot. (11.4 miles – about 18 minutes)

We will now head for **Bump Covered Bridge** which is at GPS position N 43° 48.859' W 71° 37.315'.

Head south on Hillside Dr toward US-3 N/Daniel Webster Hwy and shortly take the 1st left onto US-3 S/Daniel Webster Hwy and drive for 2.4 miles where you turn left onto Cross Rd. proceed for 0.7 miles and turn right onto NH-175 S where you drive for 7.2 miles and then continue onto Perch Pond Rd for an additional 0.4 miles. Turn right to stay on Perch Pond Rd and after 0.8 miles you will see the bridge.(11.5 miles – about 23 minutes)

Now we will head for **Blair Covered Bridge** which is at GPS position N 43° 48.616' W 71° 39.991'.

Head northwest on Perch Pond Rd and in 0.5 miles turn left onto Hogback Rd. Drive for 0.9 miles and make a slight left onto NH-175 S and then in 0.8 miles turn right onto Blair Rd where you will find the bridge in 0.7 miles. (2.9 miles – about 8 minutes)

Next stop is **Smith Millennium Covered Bridge** which is at GPS coordinates N 43° 46.517' W 71° 44.359'.

Head west on Blair Rd toward US-3 N/Daniel Webster Hwy and in 0.3 miles turn left to merge onto I-93 S   and drive 2.7 miles. Take exit 26 for New Hampshire 25/New Hampshire 3A toward U.S. 3/Plymouth/Rumney and in 0.2 miles merge onto New Hampshire 3A S/Tenney Mountain Hwy where you drive 2.4 miles and turn right onto Smith Bridge Rd. You will find the bridge in 0.5 miles. (6.2 miles – about 11 minutes)

Our final stop is 12. **Squam River Covered Bridge** which is at GPS position N 43° 43.092' W 71° 37.114'

Head southeast on Smith Bridge Rd toward Artisan Ln and after 0.5 miles turn left onto New Hampshire 3A N/NH-25 E/Tenney Mountain Hwy and continue for 2.4 miles where you take the Interstate 93 S ramp to Ashland/Concord and merge onto I-93 S. In 5.4 miles take exit 24 for US-3/NH-25 toward Ashland/Holdness and drive 0.2 miles where you turn right onto NH-25 E/US-3 S/Daniel Webster Hwy. Proceed for 2.7 miles and turn right onto River St, then another 0.1 miles and take the 1st right to stay on River St where you will see the bridge. (11.6 miles – about 17 minutes)

Self Guided Tours
Merrimack County Tour 9 Bridges - 1 hour 40 minutes driving

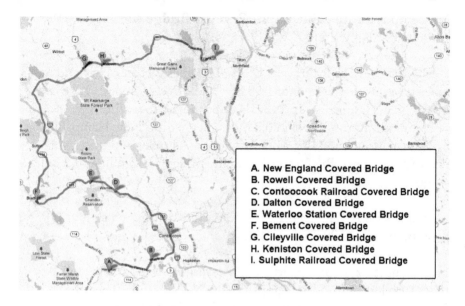

A. New England Covered Bridge
B. Rowell Covered Bridge
C. Contoocook Railroad Covered Bridge
D. Dalton Covered Bridge
E. Waterloo Station Covered Bridge
F. Bement Covered Bridge
G. Cileyville Covered Bridge
H. Keniston Covered Bridge
I. Sulphite Railroad Covered Bridge

Our tour begins at the **New England Covered Bridge** which is at
GPS position N 43° 10.646' W 71° 49.338'.
The New England Covered Bridge is found in the town of Henniker
on the New England College Campus off of US-202

Our next stop is the **Rowell Covered Bridge** is at GPS coordinates N
43° 11.539' W 71° 44.902'.

Head southwest toward NH-114 N and shortly turn left onto NH-114
N and drive 0.7 miles to take the ramp onto NH-9 E/US-202
E/Franklin Pierce Hwy E. After 3.9 miles turn left onto NH-127
N/Maple St and proceed for 0.7 miles where you turn right to stay on
NH-127 N/Maple St. Drive 0.4 miles where you will see the bridge.
(5.8 miles – about 10 minutes)

Now we will head for **Contoocook Railroad Covered Bridge** which
is at GPS position N 43° 13.375' W 71° 42.833'.

Head east toward NH-127 S/Maple St and shortly continue straight
onto NH-127 N/Maple St and after 3.8 miles you will find the bridge.

(3.8 miles – about 7 minutes)

Now we go to **Dalton Covered Bridge** which is at GPS position N 43° 16.631' W 71° 48.671'.

Head northwest on NH-103 W/Park Ave toward Kearsarge Ave and continue to follow NH-103 W for 2.9 miles and take a slight right to merge onto I-89 N. In 2.7 miles take exit 8 toward NH-103/Warner and then in 0.2 miles turn left onto Schoodac Rd. Drive 0.3 miles and continue onto NH-103 W/E Main St. In 0.9 miles turn left onto Joppa West Rd where the bridge is a short distance. (7.1 miles – about 11 minutes)

Our next destination is **Waterloo Station Covered Bridge** which is at GPS coordinates N 43° 17.302' W 71° 51.353'.

Head north on Joppa West Rd toward NH-103 E/E Main St and shortly turn left onto NH-103 W/E Main St. In 2.5 miles turn left onto Newmarket Rd and in 0.1 miles you will find the bridge. (2.7 miles – about 6 minutes)

Bement Covered Bridge is the next stop and it is at GPS coordinates N 43° 15.872' W 71° 57.161'.

Head northeast on Newmarket Rd toward Waterloo St and shortly turn left to stay on Newmarket Rd and take the 1st left onto NH-103 W. In 5.9 miles you will find the bridge. (6.0 miles – about 11 minutes)

The next stop is **Cileyville Covered Bridge** which is at GPS coordinates N 43° 25.855' W 71° 52.081'.

Head southeast on NH-103 E toward NH-114 N/Henniker Rd and in 0.2 miles turn left onto NH-114 N/Henniker Rd. Follow NH-114 N for 11.2 miles and turn right onto NH-11 E where you will find the bridge in 5.7 miles. (17.1 miles – about 26 minutes)

Keniston Covered Bridge is just a short drive and found at GPS position N 43° 26.089' W 71° 50.177'.

Head northeast on NH-11 E/Main St toward 10 Penny Ln and after 1.9 miles turn right onto Bridge Rd where you will find the bridge in 0.1 miles. (2.0 miles – about 5 minutes)

Our final stop is the **Sulphite Railroad Covered Bridge** which is at GPS coordinates N 43° 26.708' W 71° 38.119'.

Head northeast on Bridge Rd toward Northern Rail Trail - Merrimack County, and in 0.1 miles turn right onto NH-11 E/US-4 E/Main St. Drive for 1.6 miles and turn left onto NH-11 E/Franklin Hwy and after 9.9 miles turn left onto Central St. In 1.2 miles turn right onto Munroe St after 0.2 miles park and take the trail to the site as noted in the citation on the bridge.(13.0 miles – about 21 minutes)

Self Guided Tours

Sullivan County Tour 9 Bridges – 2 hours 30 minutes driving

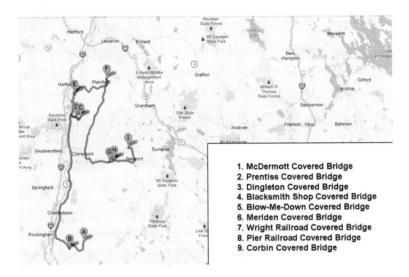

1. McDermott Covered Bridge
2. Prentiss Covered Bridge
3. Dingleton Covered Bridge
4. Blacksmith Shop Covered Bridge
5. Blow-Me-Down Covered Bridge
6. Meriden Covered Bridge
7. Wright Railroad Covered Bridge
8. Pier Railroad Covered Bridge
9. Corbin Covered Bridge

Our first stop is the **McDermott Covered Bridge** which is at GPS position N 43° 10.206' W 72° 20.744'. From the town of South Acworth go southwest on NH-123A for 3.7 miles and turn right on Crane Brook Road where the bridge is a short distance.

Our next stop is the **Prentiss Covered Bridge** which is found at GPS coordinates N 43° 09.236' W 72° 23.611'

Head south on Crane Brook Rd toward New Hampshire 123A E and after 0.1 miles take a slight right onto New Hampshire 123A W and drive for 1.3 miles. Continue onto NH-123 N/Rte 12A N/NH-12A N for 0.6 miles and turn right to stay on NH-123 N/Rte 12A N/NH-12A N, then continue to follow Rte 12A N/NH-12A N and Lower Cemetery Rd for 2.8 miles. Continue onto Cheshire Turnpike and after 0.1 miles you will see the bridge. (4.8 miles – about 10 minutes)

The next stop is the **Dingleton Covered Bridge** which is at GPS position N 43° 27.868' W 72° 22.151'.

Head north on Cheshire Turnpike for 0.1 miles and take the 1st left to stay on Cheshire Turnpike and after 0.6 miles take the 1st right toward Rte 12A N/NH-12A N and go left onto Rte 12A N/NH-12A N. In 3.1 miles turn left onto NH-12 N/Rte 12A N/NH-12A N and proceed for 8.2 miles. Turn left onto Rte 12A N/NH-12A N and after 12.5 miles turn right onto Town House Rd. In another 0.9 miles turn right onto Root Hill Rd where you will see the bridge. (25.5 miles – about 42 minutes)

Next we head for **Blacksmith Shop Covered Bridge** which is at GPS coordinates N 43° 27.770' W 72° 21.237'.

Head north on Root Hill Rd toward Town House Rd and shortly turn right onto Town House Rd. The bridge is found in 1.1 miles. (1.2 miles – about 3 minutes)

The next stop will be **Blow-Me-Down Covered Bridge** at GPS position N 43° 31.026' W 72° 22.439'.

Head southwest on Town House Rd toward Chase Hill Rd and in 2.0 miles continue onto Rte 12A N/NH-12A N. Drive another 2.5 miles and turn right onto Platt Rd and then 1.2 miles and turn left onto Lang Rd. The bridge is about 0.1 miles. (5.9 miles – about 13 minutes)

Next stop is the **Meriden Covered Bridge** at GPS coordinates N 43° 33.197' W 72° 15.922'.

Head northwest on Lang Rd and continue onto Mill Rd for 0.3 miles and turn right onto Rte 12A N/NH-12A N and after 1.4 miles turn right onto Daniels Rd. In 0.9 miles take a slight right onto Stage Rd and drive 4.8 miles turn left onto NH-120 N/Route 120 N and shortly take the 1st left onto Bonner Rd. Go 0.6 miles and turn left onto Main St where you will find the bridge in 0.5 miles. (8.7 miles – about 23 minutes)

Now we head for the **Wright Railroad Covered Bridge** which is at GPS position N 43° 21.533' W 72° 15.517'.

Head southwest on Main St toward Colby Hill Rd and after 0.5 miles turn right onto Bonner Rd and then in 0.6 miles turn right onto NH-

120 S/Route 120 S. Travel 12.5 miles and turn left onto Route 120 S and then after 0.1 miles take the 1st right onto Broad St. Go 0.1 miles and turn left onto Tremont St continuing onto Opera House Square and shortly turn right onto Broad St/Tremont St. Continue to follow Broad St and after 0.4 miles turn left onto Chestnut St. In 0.5 miles continue onto Chestnut St Exn and after 0.9 miles make a slight left onto Sugar River Dr. You will find the bridge in 3.1 miles. (18.9 miles – about 34 minutes)

Now we go to another railroad bridge, the **Pier Railroad Covered Bridge** which is at GPS coordinates N 43° 21.721' W 72° 14.520'.

Head east on Chandlers Mill Rd/Sugar River Dr toward Abandoned Railroad Grde/Sugar River Trail and go 1.0 miles and the bridge will be seen. (1.0 miles – about 3 minutes)

Our last stop is the **Corbin Covered Bridge** which is at GPS position N 43° 23.456' W 72° 11.699'.

Head southeast on Chandlers Mill Rd toward Langley Rd and after 1.1 miles turn right onto NH-103 E/NH-11 E/John Stark Hwy and continue to follow NH-103 E/NH-11 E for 2.9 miles. Turn left onto Main St and then after 0.2 miles turn left onto Sunapee St and quickly take the 1st right onto N Main St. Proceed 1.8 miles and turn left onto Corbin Rd. You will find the bridge in 0.7 miles (6.7 miles – about 16 minutes)

This is the end of our tour.

Glossary

Abutment: The abutments are the bridge supports on each side bank. Usually they were
originally constructed of stone but they have often been replaced or supplemented with
concrete through the years.

Arch: A curved timber or timber set which is shaped in a curve and functions as a support of the bridge.

Bed timbers: Timbers between the abutment and the truss or bottom chord.

Brace or bracing: A diagonal timber or timber set used to support the trusses.

Bridge Deck: The roadway through the bridge.

Buttress: Wood or metal members on the exterior sides which connect the floor beams
and the top of the truss. Used to keep the bridge structure from twisting under wind,
water and snow loads.

Camber: A planned curve in the structure to compensate for the weight of the structure.

Chord: The horizontal members extending the length of the truss meant to carry the load
to the abutments.

Dead load: The load of the weight of the bridge itself.

Deck: The pathway through the bridge used by pedestrians or vehicles.

Pier: Stone/concrete supports built in the stream bed to support the bridge

Portal: The bridge's entrances.

Post: The truss's vertical members.

Span: The bridge length measured between the abutments.

Treenails or trunnels: Pins or dowels turned from hardwood, driven into holes drilled into the members of the truss to hold them together. Also used in mortised joints.

Truss: The framework which carries the load of the bridge and distributes it to the
abutments.

Trunnels
Trunnels or Tree Nails are wooden nails used to join members

Truss Types

A Truss is a system of ties and struts which are connected to act like a single beam to distribute and carry a load. In covered bridges, these Trusses carry the load to stone abutments at each side and perhaps piers in between. Following are the most common types of Trusses used in Covered Bridges.

Kingpost

Kingpost is the simplest form of Truss with two diagonal members on a bottom chord, often with a vertical post connecting to the diagonals. The multiple Kingpost involves a series of Kingposts symmetrical from the bridges center. This allows for a much longer span.

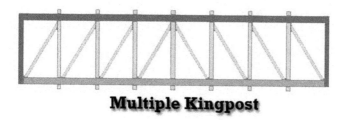

Multiple Kingpost

Queenpost

The Queenpost has the peak of the kingpost type replaced with a horizontal top chord which allows for a longer span.

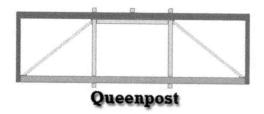

Queenpost

Long

The Long Truss was patented by Stephen Long in 1830. It is a series of X shaped diagonals connected to vertical posts.

Long

Burr Arch

Invented in 1804 by Theodore Burr, the Burr Arch is one of the most commonly found structures in Covered Bridge design. It is often used in combination with multiple kingposts. The ends of the arch are buried in the abutments.

Burr Arch

Howe

The Howe Truss was patented in 1840 by William Howe. It involves the use of vertical metal rods between the joints of wooden diagonals.

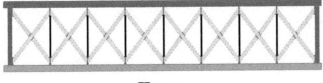

Howe

Town

The Town or lattice system was patented by Ithiel Town in 1820. It involved a system of overlapping diagonals in a lattice pattern connected at the intersection by Tree nails or trunnels, wooden pegs or dowels. It had the advantages in that it could be constructed by unskilled labor and local materials could be used.

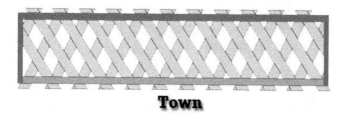

Town

Childs

The Childs Truss System is essentially a multiple kingpost with half of the diagonal timbers replaced with iron bars.

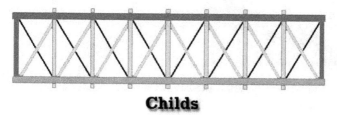

Childs

Pratt

The Pratt truss was patented in 1844 by Caleb Pratt and his son Thomas Willis Pratt. The design uses vertical members for compression and horizontal members to respond to tension.

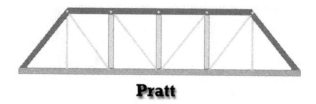

Pratt

Smith

Robert W. Smith received patents in 1867 and 1869 for variations of his system.

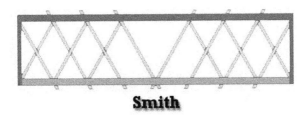

Partridge

Reuben L. Partridge received a patent for a design similar to the Smith system but adding terminal braces at the end and a central vertical member.

Warren

Patented in 1848 by two Englishmen, one of whom was named James Warren, it consists of parallel upper and lower chords with diagonal connecting members forming a series of equilateral triangles.

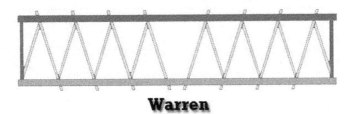

Paddleford

Peter Paddleford worked with the Long Truss system and eventually adapted it with a system of interlocking braces. he was never able to patent the system due to challenges from the owners of the Long Truss patent. However there are a number of New Hampshire and Vermont bridges which use the Paddleford system

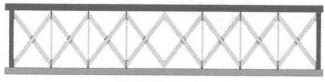

Paddleford

Brown

Josiah Brown Jr., of Buffalo, New York, patented this system in 1857.It consists of diagonal cross compression members connected to horizontal top and bottom stringers and is known for economic use of materials. It was only used in Michigan where there are a couple of surviving members.

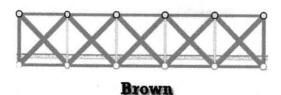

Brown

Bibliography and References

Internet sources

National Society for the Preservation of Covered Bridges
http://www.coveredbridgesociety.org

New Hampshire Historical Society
https://www.nhhistory.org/

New Hampshire Division of Historical Resources
http://www.nh.gov/nhdhr/bridges/table.html

In Print

Covered Bridges of the Northeast by Richard Sanders Allen (Dover Books on Americana) 1957

The Last of the Covered Bridge Builders, by Milton Graton (Clifford-Nicol) 1990

Covered Bridges of Vermont, Ed Barna (The Countryman Press) 2000

New Englands Covered Bridges, Benjamin and June Evans (University Press of New England) 2004

New England's Covered Bridges, Harold Stiver (Createspace) 2012

World Guide to Covered Bridges 2009 Edition, David Wright, Editor

Index

Other Books By Harold Stiver

1. New York Covered Bridges

2. Ontario's Old Mills

3. Massachusetts Covered Bridges

4. Michigan Covered Bridges

5. Connecticut Covered Bridges

6. Vermont Covered Bridges

7. Indiana Covered Bridges

8. New England Covered Bridges

9. Maine Covered Bridges

10. Birding Guide to Orkney

CPSIA information can be obtained
at www.ICGtesting.com
Printed in the USA
BVHW052117250723
667821BV00002B/22